recombinant recombinant

recombinant recombinant recombinant recombinant recombinant recombinant recombinant recombinant recombinant recombinant recombinant

Kelsey Street Press

recombinant recombinant

recombinant recombinant recombinant recombinant

recombinant recombinant

recombinant recombinant recombinant

recombinant recombinant

recombinant recombinant recombinant

recombinant recombinant recombinant

Ching-In Chen

recombinant recombinant recombinant recombinant

recombinant

recombinant recombinant recombinant recombinant recombinant recombinant recombinant recombinant

recombinant recombinant

KELSEY STREET PRESS 2824 KELSEY STREET BERKELEY, CA 94705

INFO@KELSEYST.COM WWW.KELSEYST.COM

COPYRIGHT © 2017 BY CHING-IN CHEN

LIBRARY OF CONGRESS CATALOGING-IN-PUBLICATION DATA

NAMES: CHEN, CHING-IN, 1978- AUTHOR.

TITLE: RECOMBINANT / CHING-IN CHEN.

DESCRIPTION: PAPERBACK EDITION. | BERKELEY, CA : KELSEY STREET PRESS, 2017. |
    INCLUDES BIBLIOGRAPHICAL REFERENCES.

IDENTIFIERS: LCCN 2016051684 | ISBN 9780932716866 (SOFTCOVER : ACID-FREE PAPER)

CLASSIFICATION: LCC PS3603.H4472 A6 2017 | DDC 811/.6—DC23

LC RECORD AVAILABLE AT HTTPS://LCCN.LOC.GOV/2016051684

COVER ILLUSTRATION: GERALDINE LAU, INFORMATION
RETRIEVAL 131 (CENTRAL PACIFIC RAILROAD), 2007

DESIGNED BY QUEMADURA

ant recombinant recombinant recombinant **recombinant** recombinant recombinant recombinant **recombinant** recombinant recombir
ecombinant recombinant recombinant recombinant **recombinant** recombinant recombinant recombinant **recombinant** recombinant
mbinant **recombinant** recombinant recombinant recombinant **recombinant** recombinant recombinant recombinant **recombinant** rec
ant recombinant recombinant **recombinant**

recombinant **recombinant** recombinant recombinant
mbinant recombinant recombinant recombinant **recombinant** recombinant recombinant recombinant **recombinant** recombinant rec
nt recombinant **recombinant** recombinant recombinant recombinant **recombinant** recombinant recombinant recombinant **recombir
ecombinant recombinant **recombinant** recombinant recombinant recombinant **recombinant** recombinant recombinant recombinant
mbinant recombinant recombinant **recombinant** recombinant recombinant recombinant **recombinant** recombinant recombinant rec
nt **recombinant** recombinant recombinant recombinant **recombinant** recombinant recombinant recombinant **recombinant** recombir
ecombinant **recombinant** recombinant recombinant recombinant **recombinant** recombinant recombinant recombinant **recombinant**
mbinant recombinant **recombinant** recombinant recombinant recombinant **recombinant** recombinant recombinant recombinant rec
nt recombinant recombinant recombinant **recombinant** recombinant recombinant recombinant **recombinant** recombinant recombir
ecombinant recombinant recombinant recombinant **recombinant** recombinant recombinant recombinant **recombinant** recombinant
mbinant **recombinant** recombinant recombinant recombinant **recombinant** recombinant recombinant recombinant **recombinant** rec
ant recombinant recombinant **recombinant** recombinant recombinant recombinant **recombinant** recombinant recombinant recombir
ecombinant recombinant recombinant **recombinant** recombinant recombinant recombinant **recombinant** recombinant recombinant

combinant recombinant **recombin
ecombinant recombinant **recombinant** recombinant recombinant recombinant **recombinant** recombinant recombinant recombinant
mbinant recombinant recombinant **recombinant** recombinant recombinant recombinant **recombinant** recombinant recombinant rec
nt **recombinant** recombinant recombinant recombinant **recombinant** recombinant recombinant recombinant **recombinant** recombin
ecombinant **recombinant** recombinant recombinant recombinant **recombinant** recombinant recombinant recombinant **recombinant**
mbinant recombinant **recombinant** recombinant recombinant recombinant **recombinant** recombinant recombinant recombinant rec
ant recombinant recombinant recombinant **recombinant** recombinant recombinant recombinant **recombinant** recombinant recombir

mbinant **recombinant** recombinant recombinant recombinant **recombinant** recombinant recombinant recombinant **recombinant** rec
ant recombinant recombinant **recombinant** recombinant recombinant recombinant **recombinant** recombinant recombinant recombin
ecombinant recombinant recombinant **recombinant** recombinant recombinant recombinant **recombinant** recombinant recombinant
mbinant recombinant recombinant recombinant **recombinant** recombinant recombinant recombinant **recombinant** recombinant rec
nt recombinant **recombinant** recombinant recombinant recombinant **recombinant** recombinant recombinant recombinant **recombin
ecombinant recombinant **recombinant** recombinant recombinant recombinant **recombinant** recombinant recombinant recombinant
mbinant **recombinant** recombinant recombinant **recombinant** recombinant recombinant recombinant **recombinant** recombinant recombinant rec
nt **recombinant** recombinant recombinant recombinant **recombinant** recombinant recombinant recombinant recombinant **recombinant** recombin

ecombinant recombinant recombinant recombinant recombinant recombinant recc
nt recombinant recombinant recombinant recombinant recombinant recombinant recombinant recombir
ecombinant recombinant recombinant recombinant recombinant recombinant recombinant recombinant recombinant recombinant
mbinant recombinant recombinant recombinant recombinant recombinant recombinant recombinant recombinant recombinant recc

recombinant recombinant recombinant recombinant recombinant recombinant recombinant recombinant recombinant recombinant
mbinant recombinant recombinant recombinant recombinant recombinant recombinant recombinant recombinant recombinant rec
nt recombinant recombinant recombinant recombinant recombinant recombinant recombinant recombinant recombinant recombin
recombinant recombinant recombinant recombinant   recombinant recombinant
mbinant recombinant recombinant recombinant recombinant recombinant recombinant recombinant recombinant recombinant rec
nt recombinant recombinant recombinant recombinant recombinant recombinant recombinant recombinant recombinant recombin
recombinant recombinant recombinant recombinant recombinant recombinant recombinant recombinant recombinant recombinant
mbinant recombinant recombinant recombinant recombinant recombinant recombinant recombinant recombinant recombinant recc
nt recombinant recombinant recombinant recombinant recombinant recombinant recombinant recombinant recombinant recombir
ecombinant recombinant recombinant recombinant recombinant recombinant recombinant recombinant recombinant recombinant
mbinant recombinant recombinant recombinant recombinant recombinant recombinant recombinant recombinant recombinant rec
ant recombinant recombinant recombinant recombinant recombinant recombinant recombinant recombinant recombinant recombir
recombinant recombinant recombinant recombinant recombinant recombinant recombinant recombinant recombinant recombinant

ant recombinant recombinant recombinant recombinant recombinant recombinant recombinant recombinant recombinant recombin
recombinant recombinant recombinant recombinant recombinant recombinant recombinant recombinant recombinant recombinant
mbinant recombinant recombinant recombinant recombinant recombinant recombinant recombinant recombinant recombinant rec
nt recombinant recombinant recombinant recombinant recombinant recombinant recombinant recombinant recombinant recombir
recombinant recombinant recombinant recombinant recombinant recombinant recombinant recombinant recombinant recombinant
mbinant recombinant recombinant recombinant recombinant recombinant recombinant recombinant recombinant recombinant recc
nt recombinant recombinant recombinant recombinant recombinant recombinant

mbinant recombinant recombinant recombinant recombinant recombinant recombinant recombinant recombinant recombinant rec
ant recombinant recombinant recombinant recombinant recombinant recombinant recombinant recombinant recombinant recombir
recombinant recombinant recombinant recombinant recombinant recombinant recombinant recombinant recombinant recombinant
mbinant recombinant recombinant recombinant recombinant recombinant recombinant recombinant recombinant recombinant rec
ant recombinant recombinant   recombinant recombinant recombin
recombinant recombinant recombinant recombinant recombinant   recombinant
mbinant recombinant recombinant recombinant recombinant recombinant recombinant recombinant recombinant recombinant rec
ant recombinant

island where these things (origin)

Twenty hours a day   Your mothers before you   all robot, all hand

Your streetmarket mother bear you

desert   Your rich mother sell you father

for ricebowl   heady mother with wrong-

amphibian love   deposit you in boarding school to avoid the shame-

life   This mountain grandmother coin-

operate in hallway

a captain mother sell whale bone to first museum of Americas

a stayput mother fly wisp of smoke

a starlet mother bury backyard career

a stay

at home velvet couch mother mix arsenic into cake

and off her-

self   warden's suggestion

a run to equator

end   like your father sweet

who become mother too

inspector of journals makes introductions:
Fan & Basket plot escape from Peabody Essex Museum

winter sibling mold and fire   **a birthright**
                         born with an army
line a desk   *in my father's tongue. She was one who*
build paper
drown records   *lined coats and gushed*
kept men with failing bodies

                                                      pork
                                            fat, one who fasted
                                tomatoes, sizzled without mushrooms.

Mocha, Red Sea, Lisbon, Madeira, Manila, Sumatra, India, China, Australia, Sandwich and Marquesas
Island

                              We marveled often at his dissolving
                                      mouth, hard
                                        sweat on pan,

this matchmaker of tiny details

                                   crafted no inheritance

                                        but what teeth procured, familiar

young man   *dark between lips*

of bitten seas

dear nightpeople we couldn't ferry

on our backs   *Who* do you

              chant   *calm and*

east

do you leave   *open stream,*

       this nightnews   *wide palm receive*

skindoor   intact

      constrict   *How many*

stretch, how many   *windless*

      names beyond

draw

dark   porch penny

river   heat

your name   in windy grass

           Who contain door

     within another, who listen   make almost light

        breathe careful key

     If body folds into I

do you terrain and safe

     my whole life and life before   wonder

deep heart   now who

          move through world, warm

sun and all days branch out   *If repeat machine*

Who   *quicksilver heart flash*
  recognize

                          Breath and breath   *filling*

guilt body   *over and over*   *faucet not stop run*

                     A wink   *move street*
                     make small

tree grow deep   *settle home*
                     made   *A repeat sweet*
                                                         machine

to construct a ghazal

Conductor's bright sentences strung in light of morning
My eyes still bold though deep ice of full morning.
The workers small particles like dried branches from crumbled tree
We accumulate loose mass of metal each night until morning.
He tells me to crumple our careful leaves like city trash
Our scaffolding unborn and lost to judging sea one future morning.
A synthetic weave wears refugee down crowded street.
I fall again from unequal distribution uprooted into mourning.
Against ground when they ask me what my name
No memory what I held in my mouth that bright morning.

[Dear Grand Avenue:

where Lee Chung's   where Wah Lee's

                              theft complains theft

fall 1885, police detectives find your little

                        Auction hall conversation, a white girl

                                    transaction scatters bed

                        mob and map render to use]

dear basket,

(possibly Twana/Coast Salish #E3624)

They say your salt vein captain snatch

gilded East Wind.
Couldn't see his rust
gate breath

                                        navigate circular tongue

swim around
him—whale
oil, bone crunch.

From one daylight woman
to another, I want

skin

fan
(1835-1850 #E9631)

                                        *

                              island where these things (deposit)

                                                grip cash teeth
                              bake future   threat eggs
                                        safe legs deliver

                                        question bring payment
                                                call next belly

                                        details pass inspection

how open heart

Surname	Given Name	Age	Sex	Race	Relationship to Head	Occupation	Location	Rent or Owned?
					against interests			
flicker								
small notes reply we								
					open would be			

Throat

heritage

When   "To say" a woman
become monument "in front of all these people"
                             never sang porridge songs
or pull   by my hair
         into line   she place
         me row by row   "men and boys"   black heads "surging"
         uncover production   "in knots of half a dozen or more"

I became not her stone
"who have paid money for their wives"

she "reckless"   stood tremble
in fire
                       "get a rope" say the crowdface

"regular traffic"
"black with people"   stare her down
             "the little mite"
             corridor   "a good many times"
                         "the unprintable" "sneak[ing]"
                                       "advance a foot"

                                 "string
                                   them up
to a lamp
                                       post"

                                                                    dear story of a

risk,

1878. I found them in box. Wright's Directory of Milwaukee. Their printed
names dusty on page. Shane Ring 276 3d. Wing Wau, 86 Mason. Clean as
sheet, near in their rows. Shelved,

                                         a thin woman's back *attempting to see*
covered, paths cut off.

                                         as if war on skin *[how many left behind*
                                         this book] and paper this sergeant
                                         this gunmaker she says *I do not want a window*
                                         in the fucking sky.

                                         *

dear fan,
            (1835-1850 #E9631)

What if typhoon
ground a long look brother in good earth?

Your painted reflections captured
by each gold eye

His eye must have fit into my belly,
your captain's pleasure name
also made of bone.

basket,
            (possibly Twana/Coast Salish #E3624)

census: x

11th quadrant 19 years   **june 6.**   *First bill of sale, this city found over counter.*

               People of this city born,

               rows and eyes   *push*

give way   male and another   *rotten vegetable sea, all direction water*

conjoin water and land female   paths

               cut off   wring prayer

daily in wood   *You too hidden in truck cheek head into coast*

.

out of backroom fear   same   *border a question.*

occupation   rent home

             A tour guide

two years in sea   brother

read, write, and speak commerce tongue

     across a body one year apart

       say you   burn this home dusty on page

an origin year   *called a border*

     slab by slab

[Dear Third Street:

where old world Chen Quen
　　　　contends influx laundryman
scours and sees a 203 Third Street adult

　　　　　　　　　　has 2 names

　　　　　　　　　　　　Superintendent Whitehead laundries a white

Business District wife

　　　　　　　"Jim Young" a sour business and residence]

dear basket,

Story is each curio
witch seed

artifact breath.

What possession

but desire to hold
a body frozen

in ground. Brothers lost

trade

stations, punish sky
root in baggage

sent home. Tell me
this isn't

so.

yours,
fan

*

**letter for export
(june 6)**

Dear C -

sin.   a pear. *City*
full of pilgrim, looking for plague.
Each carried diary, noting down who settled what.
Wait to be incorporated, write in my own longhand.

Sincerely,
Golden Venture, New York

oral history revisited: interview with assistant

after Michael Lin

Each house curves a may-open story if you follow his way. Do not open touch-up doors. Some days each empty family get magnify, get reproduce. Under blue pattern, specific parameter. Only within my limits, our glazed family under spotlights. Place myself in pattern of protection. Brother bright and bent over each small man, kiss belly and grip, each whiskey put off to sea. Dream door came

open in my hand, dream you open my hand, back rose in air, no limit to our small men empty, your back free of payments, your brother in doorway, grows teeth at dawn.

[Dear Fifth Street:

if Hah Ding's laundry

Clara Kitzkow

evidence other
girls (laid
beside) "to visit"

question

to tie flesh]

how heart open [32 feet of chain, undecipherable]

CHAW	FRANK	37	M	CHIN	HEAD	LAUNDRY	21-WD	R
LAW	ASIA	30	M	CHIN	HEAD	COOK	9-WD	R
LEE	PHINA	40	M	CHIN	LODGER	COOK	11_WD	R
LEE	NORM (FUN)	42	M	CHIN	HEAD	LAUNDRY	6_WD	R

one would not wish this Widowed account   *incomplete archive sharing every*

complaint,

down river	
	an incorrect thought, *recombinant.*

What that means, she asks.   goodbyes, I curl

Be *come a cat* *alog* *ue* *of this dis* *appeared*	tong ue.	*List* *en,* *list* *en, list* *en.*

skin push you & *warning?* next city. *They could bring influence to bear on a man.*

blueprint

The day
you cross line,

somebody else's ideas.

hold two
stories, red-faced

navigation, meridians. which tunnel highest prosperity point.

take bed before dusk

my government
name, form path

self-preserve.

mouth
make alternative vein.

You begin say
sorry all the way.

dear fan,

Future rooted in this

story. Each sea layer, crowd,

desire elsewhere.
Wild pepper seed and women, this city

leads to
burn, mirage.
Two towns countries at war

with all their street finery
on display 1 2 5 voyages

and still.

yours,
basket

*

basket,

In this town, you speak

prophecy. Sweet calf

glove, soft freckle
and lace. A stomach

devour disease,
a gentleman's white lies

along the road. Who we
exchange in meantime.

yours,
fan

good life. Dress plainly. Moth avoid lightning, dusk burnish gongs. One foot in front fills
pot. Friend tells me,

other side enter

transactions   *"strange stories" "hanging*
                                from a death-dealing ... dressed
                                in blue" "shuddered" "trophy"

prosper, forward   *"the face, an ashen white"*
                                "eventually spend one day
                                and one night" "congregate"
                                "around collar and body"
                                "besieged in Wisconsin"

Sun hides season   everything gather pick dry
                                "a stuffed together
                                apparition" "simmering

by time done arrives, dusted, sated
                        with hours. Pickled
                                developments" "imposed

birds outside my door   pennies
                                movement controls"
                                line up a jar. Daughter
                                "stretching across four
                                days" "committed"

                                "threatening letter"
                                we turn a corner, how
                                you *"prisoner within"*
                                at ready, body city-full.
                                "discipline"

                                "what looked like a man"
                                "tendencies"

strain, maybe. Some days, a line isn't

enough to hold.

Re-context. I've tried to notate simple things too. Ashes on page lift to fingers. Years rush by. All evidence have no paths. Give way once, another female wring slabs, burn wood stories down.

one testimony (m. Lao)

(A)   conceive on metal and leather

                     scrap   by time I born

                                     phoenix

                     sculpture weigh a ton

                                         this mother a regular

                              worker   sing belly

              air-full   hulk

                   above workers, boot

from town to town gather   outside city   this father

                             conduct unlike anything whole

               enterprise   only visit worksite

        Mondays Wednesdays and   seen except on stage

       Fridays inspect operation

progress   he initially think her shorn

                    become 12 ton remnant

                 hair smooth face   some boy he bring   12 in line around

          world

                           abroad long ago

demolition and debris

steel and beam   gifts to remark on how

            lovely   like drinking

            tears   how remarkable migrant

                     sweat   how kind

     isn't why they start

            bring mother little food

when she stop

       talk   her mouth

     No one—shed a flaking skin— I'm no one they've seen

                                      before.

(B)   Conductor watch   Mother's hands socket wrench
              I track orchestra   as wood root and curve
                                                    wear down floor

        plate molt and balcony steel

        when minutes complete halve and flake circle
                    center workpile heart

                                                Years later, shed
                    eyes, travel country: risk they-child's paid-for
                                                        lungs, risk frost-tongue
              to eat, risk
                        build this empire (containers,
                                    oyster sauce, skinshelves,
                    mobius) on basement sand.

Face up from sanitize hands, peel and pain, shake and shred. Ash, they sigh and repeat.

(C)   What I leave—city hot breath—not
                a mystery; mother raise no fool.

                                What opportunity come
        For sin-
child, abandon in mint
        economy. They all know

                I raise for export, bred on apple peel and rice gruel.

Old-timers say, learn history (demolition and debris), make commerce (recycle tears, traffic
sweat), empty your own mouth over each border.

(D)   Conductor bear me when mother leave

         every night flee into cold-room museum   rehearse next productive day

    (phoenix make melody
                this elder not teach
                counterpoint origin
      love someone not interest in
        body

   hang in air   not hold your weight in ground)

             All he know   mother's metal bed worn
                         hide
hair-lost head   mouth
        eventually
   close   every night

      I chase stinkstreet stomach
      pain aware   undersurface growth   sweat mire

Last night he pelt walls liquor-fill glass   shake head all time

I pin self onto floor   pleasure
barter   into his unwilling arms another
                        day   another sun
                                Two eggs break ice-floor

 Newchild born share bothface and conductor
won't talk to me   shed
        daughter into they-child
                plant stubborn inside

this father's beast thighs

                        skin   pad throat
                                miniature bite This disobedient

                body blame its furnace

They-child I lead through taxis and luxuriant
        unown rooms search for what

flesh's barter produce   To house
        within its corridors within its night

vision   This thigh
translate to onion (forty cent), this shoulder

                                  to melon (ninety-nine), this soft

                    to hide (first time, one hundred), this table

        to bite.

They-child I watch telltale
        sign peelage, skin

slippage into rot

        layer. They-child never

            do, they-child keep

    intact, skin and eye

                    firm. This tight painkiller,
                     this worker army

        produce memory from garbage.

(E)   A compress child flake day by day   your skin
                          unnatural down as if stick

                  They don't remark on it   they watch this mother string up
                          shovel and hard hat   old sewing

                                                  machine

                                                        plastic into phoenix carcass

They watch conductor circle solar monster   face quiver pleasure and disgust
             That day she fall from fake blue sky   he interview foreign press

                                      Migrant sweat
                          he repeat   and value of junk

A side illustrator sketch conductor's spider fingers
                                                                          heavy-grain

face   Before black
and white solemn workers' photograph

                              This photograph survive her, only woman (though shorn,

hairless) in a field of men.

They-child ask me   Lineage, they say,
photograph memory.   as if explain.

                              Days misplace living in gardener-run-fortress
after they-child
walk into air

                                                                    Do not return

machinery run without me   assemble perfection render obsolete.

                        Time period don't know which pockets
                        fall into, which wine
                                    balance surface, which open glass
                                            leave for others, which visitors

receive, who can't remember, which
                    dissolving powders mix

toxin, I survive and photograph vanish.

All my prized hair fall down.

My only function

                                (hidden

                        as grocery store maven),

                        fund provider (gangless

                        boy leader), action

                                origin (smuggle and traffic).

This body organize itself

                efficient, teach me survive. This body

                        manufacture relations—sister

                                thigh, brother

                eye, another son bare

                                as paper. I sell

                them this name, they begin

                                        crosswire, that mother

now piecemeal, mystery father once

fame and print elsewhere.

Nobody come to ask

question even

when they-child surface

missing. Follow official

report deliver door to door, even sell

from my high-ladder perch, only undead

trace, only evidence of this lineage.

In this swamp, metal bars, directions don't matter.

(F)   Look, each story shit another

                      nest. Phoenix travel
              sea, bear goodwill in 1 2 directions.

                    Invited to accompany[1]
          originating
              structure, speak in its creature
                          voice, give howl
                                to conductor's compassion.

---

[1]Eat
                  Nothing
first
days.   Each
          month,   push
                  natural
                  egg, shed
                        to center

    grind, gnash. Feed

        them preen,
        shine, reach
             toward skin.

I board this vessel, sign up for my payment.

Every monster has a snail

(G)   to mother bring me food (persimmon,

    cart back north, along with no use value   clementine, pear juice)

to sooth; those

inclined

judge (heavy pig blood chunks, marrow

spectacle, ghost-seed within me.   clot) to appease.

She say, nothing go from soil, nothing grow from seed.

Each payment birth payment.

Conductor leave this ticket and this photograph

                                                    In hot blood city, seed

watch over me. They feed cash register when no patron cross threshold,
                                        bring grinding sauce to correct

                                shelf. Pour bamboo
                    into spigot, cut beansoak

                                into milk, sweep flake from bed.

(H)   No one find they-child

                                        headless wire
                        perforate skin. Billyclubs

            bear my name. Some

                                        burn water,   body slip
            river, face
                        they-child surface a home for fish.

            smooth and shorn blow

                                        up grain.
                                                They-child enter

                                                        channel, if only
            No one snitch, no one pay.

(I)   They-child never return

         in this version. As if world
                peel them
            down, greet morning
             air.

Hours before, wait

         for secretary distant
             morning horizon. These twenty years, uniform
                  to please. Regardless,
                        count up hours

                  owe, minutes
               borrow offshore sex.

               Who you spend whole life love? Ask secretary
as gardener escorts himself

off compound. Love price

        strip

        belongings, one body ship

off continent, one body remain to empty the song.

(J)   Account produce ghosts:

As if two sips of water save fourteen jumping into eight hour bunk beds, two sips of water collect

muscle for payment. As if they-child would not leave. Alkaline and ridge. They-child cannot be imprint into native informant. They will not come back into any recognizable form. As if narrative from my sketchy notes—throatless tongue in court of law become no-memory faces.

They testify all against me as if my body bears theirs.

      14. 300. 200,000.

      58 airtight truck, June.
      Several teeth in gun barrel.

      Punctured territory, intestines of children buyers.
      Middlemen board house, pack fruit, counterfeit DVD.

      Cigarettes arrange wages.

As if chain command hierarchy leads to 18 sleeping in flame processing sterile.

      Farm out minibuses. Incoming tide drowners sue for compensation.

      Sugarcane pig daddies close vent.
      Canoes set up and burn shop.

(K)   As if city of cabbage make leatherskin egg.

        If sulphur, ammonia.

        Seven pounds of clay.
        Wood ash.
        Sea salt.

        Quick lime.
        Rice hulls.

As if gate I lift tomorrow pickles tea tightly. Metal, small key.
In dark before sun, let root harden, sit between teeth.

        Oil, noodle, ginger, spice packet for boiling
        chicken happy family. No cabbage milk here, no leatherskin permit. But morning
        quicklime comfort

can be approximated, impersonated.
        Three passports.

(L)   Thursday, flat machete side.

Bird visits from future, bought
        for hanging. (demolished)

will be tear from balcony, lost skin seeds. No one wear them.

                Each sent a letter in its name.
                This head needs a help.

                This handcuff asks for 2 liquid sips.
Became winter in morning. Money from machete summer sent prey, become airport.

                        At marathon's end, I do not apologize in terminal. Ask pregnant prosecutor,

(M)   What will you one year apart

        understand once   eyes give way   lungs hard to read
        you shed   body a blot
        that child

      Your name listed twice, once male, another female.

Same occupation, wringing out of backroom fear,

prayer daily in wood. Conjoin

                    water and land

next

In harbor, can't say what happen next.
My doorway brother I didn't recognize.
Sentence roll on in rain.
Captain turn his back, shoulder stretch to place,
face melt from pattern. No history here.
Between them, mouths wet with river, glass bodies.
Nothing specific tie me, our mother's
smile I put out to sea familiar. I place myself,
my payments, luck through

doorway. Under blue

sky,

mesh bone and bud,
then boat.

diagram a ghost

in January, I was a girl
not a city
streetless and star remote

       friends whistle me up
       in my wolf cap
       saw me and my ceiling
       for rescue

I whittle down my cheekbones

we joyride
flash and cried I couldn't
be a boy that heard the news
the next daylight
lay swollen
nameless feet march up
       demand my name
       be crunched in each mouth
           remorseful bite
           full of fist

composition

I want to know how to make myself color. Wassily Kandinsky looked sideways, then the sky.

sitting still. First time she
home away, instrument
pour voice, will she
remember different city
we walk muggy
summer road. Years   *Don't look at my mouth, she said.*
later, memory alters   *It doesn't make my decisions.*
something eyeless. We took a
small scar around island and
that's how we knew—we were meant to walk together partway.

A straight sentence, music disobey eardrum.

origin

rough trade. *settlers ap-*
pear on scene, explore surroundings,

day
proceed to make

a spine, as our family visit
themselves at home.

This is also how

give my government name

conventional
history books begin. Other cities,
a tree and pass

I can write in dark and sound so like myself, I could be mistaken for a city
solemn resolutions

mouth form

plaster against wall. I'm dug deep and there's not much left, even for one.

path

1884–1913. Dear unknown foot setter. Dear cook visiting as Wisconsin State Fair stove company product demonstrator. Dear lonely 16 hours and six days. Dear lonely heathen deed. Dear does not believe in advertising. Dear lonely rat eater. Dear good people are you aware. Dear lonely opium addict. Dear 3,000 men in 12 hours. Dear damage. Dear municipal court. Dear joss house display. Dear Immanuel Presbyterian church missionaries. Dear colored shirts. Dear night shirts. Dear apple pie feast with roast chicken, beef and pork. Dear hired carriages. Dear chosen picnic ground—Union Cemetery. Dear rare day of leisure. Dear fancy goods and teas. Dear "enticing," dear "immoral purposes," dear public anger. Dear March 11, 1889.

open heart how

city of last shout

NOTE: DOB 1865

CHAW	FRAN K		37	M	CHIN	HEAD	LAUN DRY	21-WD	R		
	LAW	ASIA		30	M	CHIN	HEAD	COOK	9-WD	R	
	LEE	PHINA		40	M	CHIN		LODG E F		11-WD	R
	NORM	FUN	LEE		42	M		CHIN	R		

street where

SINGLE

things ghost a body

1883

YR IMMIGRATE

17 YRS LAUNDRY

CAN READ, WRITE & SPEAK ENGLISH

to bullet

Don't waste your time replace her scrapped arm with fragrance, *Master unit with lock brake*
she exit lighter than she came.

                  who crash lightning
             who burn our feet to print
                  hang on trees try live as if true:

[Dear Chestnut Street:

where Joseph   *bone a Chinese laundry @ 1pm*
                                                        Caspari's saloon lynched 618 Chestnut
body up   *saloon street > 2 Chinese*

future artifacts   *on Winnebago Street   Caspari's*
men escape windows   *where 618 Chestnut*

             and excavate]

to diagram [the ghost did not] city

A NOTED CONFESSIONAL: I can't write   DOB

birds of avenues with no trees   [no origin], YR IMMIGRATE [alters]

[X] YRS IN US, rebind CAN LAUNDER, RECITE CHAW   scrapped a 40 contaminant

AND TESTIFY   Married books shaking houses

    [ex. A city cleans dirt, wipes fingerprint on boat.

    We asked only to

        complete proper usage—lacunae LEE]

[to house a ghost]	s/he yr immigrant birds with no trees
when yr chaw scrapped when yr books contaminant	shaking widowed houses
then she says yellow city clean as dirt	then radio host with all his boats wipes fingers
teaches lacunae last name LEE and CHAW	no avenues but write no sings but FUN
LEE for sure has epidermis proper complete	animal voice exfoliated and locked

	as brake hangs tree		
		last I heard, s/he lived in	
ungrateful house contracted fire			
		syllable skin	
			no one could verify
though knockers parked outside door			recitations
	early morn, during hot-tot lunch		
		evenings wet with questions	
			administered
counters said		quizzes must be	
until houses exit			
	until boxes forget		
exfoliate and goose			nobody sings
			head grow evidence

letter for export
(September 1)

Somewhere in Boston   loom   a shrunken kidney   each white field
                                                           your secure catalogue

    lonely bathroom man
    blue a fabricated sour

Organs have their own intelligence, she says.

                    deduct pattern. contract livelihood. Shame
                        my father's heir

        Later, in interrogation room, a line of evidence, a swath of code.

                                                        Earnestly,
                                                Posse & March, Selma

ghost of a diagram

city generates birds
        who pour complete
        who immigrant trees
        who dirt the body
    clean as cedar
    white as machine   we decorate our face to night
                to compose each family

        without contracting
           underground fire
    last I heard
    s/he drench the ground a liquid
        if not careful
        could lose your sight
           though your mouth

that mouth
    will never sleep

*

island where these things (knock-off)

        paper currency grow built-
        eye night
        bed business
    microphone cleanse paper fluid
        strung up plastic
        recycle yo-yo wood
        into drumstick synthetic lace

    discard travel knob after one washing use

heavy suns flood market

sunrise. If "no people in the true sense of the word" is mutated cartography of island. Then shipwreck, then borderman. Egg an 11th quadrant machine. A production of feed back—rent home:: repeat ::

a seething in sea lay down detour and archipelago. Not-quite past is brother can read. He machine then, he wind then.

Produce coast, home not yours. Secrete slab on map, each sideways smooth. Night by night, that murky territory when doorknob loose, blue men come through. In morning, demand for who missing, who substitute, who grow.

f —

What he needed from me I have no idea.
So I spread blood rumors out
front, stuck them
cedar spines high,
shifted their bird locations,
let out to wind,
to ghost, to surface streets.
I saw you wooden box,
microscope, visitor
eye rolled down
into coinbox collection.
What do you think
of me now?

b

*

letter for export
(october 18)

dear sea captain ancestor
    opium trade ancestor
        what you own ancestor
           store up prisoners ancestor
      unroll family cabinet ancestor
          war machine daddy

I imagine you father   Forbes

"You not pilgrim. Why you think you pilgrim!" Face a storm, father coming to drench me
down.

A real possibility,
Lynch & Knife, Los Angeles

war

Sister in-between, orange danger. Hips sway, feet stomp   gold rush.

                                                    remember that lightning. I practice

hiss, we form

boat in night,
jaguar.   Which correction mob form vigilante.

String wire *in half.*

            somebody else's ideas. Before me, body rang curling voice, island milk,
            oil splatter. Were you easy and burnt, light feet one and two, never settle basket,
            your mother a breath taken by sea, land, freight.

what light heart sit high
another envious morning
pass other
bodies lonely
to bear rain

            Unit must survive. Draw sunrise, call obey, who wild. *I say, all paths begin in water.*

                                                    I say, what learned—

                                        Girl on
                              synthetic girl, push
                              me down to dirt.
                                        Mating ritual
                              [braid, stomach, hair
                              follicle,
                                                grow silent

metal, something to
  sliding hands] begin
  last

if our breath manufacture

sometimes even this ending
      "congregate" "around collar and body"

          lit lineage. High in air, raise a girl bomb. To pluck, along neck, breath. Under water, I cannot burn her down with matches bent to orange.

then sharks break
small men upon door

                         a path   *In summer,*
                     ground down   *moth-selves*
                             a small
                       fish with all teeth

        burn windows   Intact parasite
                                 then go hunt
                              spartan
                              ancestors.

                                    we be
                          next weed to
                                      fly

[as a space to occupy] crossing the source

mash-up harvest from/in response to words & images of Michael Lin & Nick Cave

in history of skin composition, my mother floats sea

                                        I—I stitch story from your *switchboard* birth mouth

ransack which hair   sentence cannot hold your *no operator*

                                                   chorus midst a sugar   brother

the one in charge of flight

      born of paper

          a code father made of grains   pages keep no mailslot letter bodies

if I—I take your tongue, I ask for his name

         he pushes her shoulder past starting line

                      no exits town

only hair stitch on my tongue

         each unchain sentence know no limit

they hold outlets under sea

        She could have her own memory To translate :

                   Floating surface containers

            polarized muscle full /thrift museum

in your forage/eye border
                300 of a thing provoke
                                itself as keyhole
        but her eye belong

in each ransack morning
I obscure exits

        procedure to ransack sentence
                each sentence intimate with her chain of command

                        her hold onto book   each stroke
infected with sperm   a roof split at river

        distance town
                letters through mailslot
notice enforce silence
        her mouth a river in place

                no guests spare chain
        separate horizon from infection

What composes town   this neck
                lace dark owl
        a kill cave
                burst
flower

                                two discard
                muscle and neck compose
        skin

                we dance two letters   one

story lose ladder

I never really work alone

      She whisper full and soft

             two rivers into keyhole

a ship make public

      highway original live as skin

                    Two continents stitch each other shut.

hunting ancestors

brittle words
so concerned   bottom rivers

                      ironcast
           pot

She walk backwards   hard
to open   A friend
                 tells me, I could

your fingers, but there

      write poems, I
think. Difficult

in light, graceful

     gathering season, everything pick dry. Hungry,   my door

                   step. We
              pickle birds
                outside
              turn a
         corner, how you

       strain, maybe.
       Some days, a line

a lit ghost

winter made me 18 shots a January city ghost   no trees become clear of immigrant

            don't tell me who contracts the dawn

                        no fingerprint speaks to risk the sun   with all their
whistle-up boys

            don't tell me who shot the drought

                                    with all their flash-
thin voices

            don't tell me who clears the coming

                                    with all their pigskin
 sold stories

            who smooths their cheeks
            who turns out to break the news

f —

Tension in the air, pair of black
boots, pink-eyed horses, my mother's
hands limp against her thigh.

Prisoners bend over
like great white sails,
their black and brown hands,
their male bodies held no language
of their own, a red handprint,
fallow season of autumn
looking at a tree. All the women
had gold teeth, hearts like withered
raisins. I began to run,
the mirror was broken.

b

*

island where these things (if this beginning)

Forget when aliened from this house.
Teeth and heart plant origin story too.
New metal millennium woman, ferrets bucket
by bucket to certified shore.

Everyone need proper. Witness hands journey into midnight.

Learn gravity, watch how she collect
ears, starting with your own.

dear island letter writer,

Once I held onto her glass
voice, my mother a sentence

pour into book's
mouth, each spider
in pages stretch
into place.

My mother eat river,
mouth rain-fill.

Do not repeat past,
she kiss me, my face
wet with procedure.

I step to next
harbor.

[Dear Jefferson:

where laundryman despite what

                                     during worst of riot (@ Huron)

                 I don't want forget   ]

                            didn't dare leave pleasure

       here

closed sky

Morning rose empty
as pigeon, beak
on horizon.
     Cleanse.
Someone else, another body
cooks in dense air.

What song lives each
time sun goes out.

Lightbulbs then, wood
oil flames.

  *

Someone cleans sea.
A body fragrant in air breaks
molecules and surface.

This body cleans
surface. A song comes
out to peck and pray.

Sun feeds on prey.
Make body alight
Rest thing which
can't stay
infection

*

A pathogen cleans fragrant
body. Eats
skin, repeats song
in infected moring.

Whatever abnormal has
no story. I composed
my host and what they
replicate. I fear
only to repeat.

    *

sun feeds this coat

An envelope of protein.
A surrounding system
of damage. A host
makes body light
and break.

    *   *

Look, no one cleans sea. Their surface recombines with dirt. Molecules another bird.
Pathogen in morning
song insect flying into sun

    *

Look, sea does not want to participate. No one on side of sea.

Oilslick mouth is a her.

What does not close is a skin next to skin.

Drops of birds come to host

to become diagram

a January city become immigrant
clears complete fingerprints

no houses have girls
who whistle up boys
        flash their feet south
        thin out voices
        bleed out their pigs

who grin and bear their changing hands
        their growing breasts
        their smoother cheeks

this city turns up to turn out
        breaks the news to pieces
        when they hear what stories sold

*

island where these things (seed)

in this flashskin house   our oldchain object lives
ears may not friend   a closet rent-full no hands
listen but fathers rise yellow
B flat tongues incubate pearl mouth song
birds bear discordant boat chords
cargo ceilings yank downstream

various various

Not what the captain recorded.

    *

My mother bought—
       India's west coast, fort wall shoulder
       a thousand everyday hands
       cutting clay to put on table

    *

cities gather to watch divisions *To know absolutely there will be an end to this relationship—apart from keepsakes.*

    *

       after loud journey and birds

    *

die. Suddenly,

       imperial decree   forced boulevard resurrection

    *

Enclaves in english factory ports

    *

        mouth like a hull
        two teeth cracked to sigh

    *

Years later, I opened book, wooden box for treasure, captured lines sank gently to floor.

    *

only approachable on foot
network of cities   water tanks

    *

Stories of this pillar road which ate and ate through ears, toe stubs. I avoided road in my walk to market; a carriage pushed me off home road. Follow tributary into marked section, recently emptied of plague. There were stories.

    *

Book begins with epigraph: "every body that is not my body is a foreign country." Then the water tank a growth I paid for with my eye.

    *

Though map muddy, I forced my sore body through pane-glass hedge. Measured air in my mouth. I missed my eye.

    *

Caption—no ear belongs here.

diagram: early coroner's songbird

island where these ghosts
a salt dress shorn
a body chrysalis
turned to bullet and dance
twist and shout
your last name could be mine
could be a moor

                                          printed on your anklet

*

island where these things (asylum)

what does liberation   *what does self-determination*
     squat cornerstores of the world   *get ready*

"inspector of journals makes introductions: *Fan & Basket plot escape from Peabody Essex Museum*/a birthright": Fan and Basket reference two artifacts in the collection of the Peabody Essex Museum in Salem, Massachusetts. This sequence of poems borrows language from Anne Carson, Jeanette Winterson, Linda Hogan, Muriel Rukeyser and Terrance Hayes.

"how open heart," "how heart open [32 feet of chain, undecipherable]," and "open heart how": use borrowed language from Srikanth Reddy, Keith + Mendi Obadike, Selina Tusitala Marsh, "10 Steps to Loving Others," US manuscript census as inputs.

"heritage" and "good life/other side enter": Italicized words from Victor Jew's "'Chinese Demons': the Violent Articulation of Chinese Otherness and Interracial Sexuality in The U.S. Midwest, 1885-1889."

"blueprint/navigation, meridians" and "origin": Italicized words from "Conclusion: How to Study the Landscape" by J. B. Jackson.

"sunrise": I came across James Anthony Froude's statement that the Caribbean had "no people in the true sense of the word" in Shalini Puri's "Canonized Hybridities, Resistant Hybridities: Chutney Soca, Carnival, and the Politics of Nationalism."

"war/somebody else's ideas": while watching Ananya Dance Theater's Kshoy!/Decay!

"various various": Italicized words from Daniel Borzutzky's *The Book of Interfering Bodies*, Kimiko Hahn's *The Artist's Daughter*, Shalini Puri's "Canonized Hybridities, Resistant Hybridities: Chutney Soca, Carnival, and the Politics of Nationalism."

Grateful acknowledgment to the editors and staff of the following publications, where earlier invocations of these poems and stories appeared:

Adrienne, An Alphabet of Embers: an Anthology of Unclassifiables, BARZAKH, Better: Culture and Lit, Black Warrior Review, Court Green, Dusie, EDNA, Indiana Review, Mead Magazine, Mission at Tenth, Original Plumbing, Raed Leaf, Spoon River Poetry Review, Valley Voices, and *When We Become Weavers: Queer Female Poets on the Midwestern Experience.*

Deep gratitude to the writers, artists and scholars who encouraged, engaged with and inspired early drafts of this work, especially Brenda Cárdenas, Maurice Kilwein-Guevara, Sukanya Banerjee, Kumkum Sangari, Cary Gabriel Costello, Kimberly Blaeser, Arijt Sen, Meena Alexander, Kimiko Hahn, Joseph Legaspi, Tamiko Beyer, Carina Gia Farrero, Soham Patel, Shanae Aurora Martinez, Chelsea Wait, Lee Abbott, Victor Jew, Susu Pianchupattana, K Bradford, Ashaki Jackson, Trish Salah and Janet Carr.

These poems evolved in conversation with those I encountered at Can Serrat, Ragdale Foundation, the Norman Mailer Center, Virginia Center for the Creative Arts, Las Dos Brujas and Dickinson House. In addition, the ongoing writing communities I belong to—Kundiman, Voices of Our Nations Arts Foundation, Macondo, The Watering Hole, Callaloo, Lambda—have sustained and nurtured my writing.

Respect and appreciation to Mg Roberts, Anna Soteria Morrison, Patricia Dienstfrey and all at Kelsey Street Press.

And, of course, for Cassie, who reminds me that sometimes putting down the pen is the next step in dreaming.

Ching-In Chen

is the author of *The Heart's Traffic* (Arktoi Books/Red Hen Press) as well as co-editor of *The Revolution Starts at Home: Confronting Intimate Violence Within Activist Communities* (South End Press, AK Press). A Kundiman, Lambda, Callaloo and The Watering Hole Fellow, they are part of the Macondo and Voices of Our Nations Arts Foundation writing communities. They have also been awarded fellowships from Can Serrat, Millay Colony for the Arts, the Norman Mailer Center and Imagining America. Their work has appeared in *The Best American Experimental Writing*, *The &NOW Awards 3: The Best Innovative Writing*, and *Troubling the Line: Trans and Genderqueer Poetry and Poetics*. They are a senior editor of *The Conversant* and poetry editor of *Texas Review*. They currently teach creative writing and world literature at Sam Houston State University.